Becoming Strong in the Lord During and After Divorce

By

Cheryl Major Brandon, Ed.D.

Xulon
PRESS

*Becoming Stronger in the Lord During and
After Divorce*
*My Story of God's Keeping and Strengthening Power
Through His Word*
by Dr. Cheryl Major Brandon

Printed in the United States of America

ISBN 9781622301751

www.xulonpress.com

Introduction

The purpose of this book is to encourage Christian women who have, will have and maybe are currently going through a divorce (without the desire for divorce) while serving God. I pray that no one would ever have to experience divorce, but divorce will happen as long as this planet rotates until the Lord Jesus returns. We also know that divorce will happen because of the many times it is addressed in the scripture. It would take a fool not to acknowledge the fact that God allowed the requirements for divorce to be explained in His holy text in both the Old and New Testaments. This is not to dismiss the fact the God hates divorce but He knew the fallen nature of man would possibly need reasons for divorce so He placed those reasons in His Testaments!! The only way to overcome is to remember what the Bible has to say about the matter of overcoming: "they overcame him by the Blood of the Lamb and the word of our testimonies" (Rev. 12:11).

Many may believe that overcoming is only about overcoming sickness, financial problems, ministry problems, and death of loved ones. Overcoming also includes overcoming the trial, emotional scars, rejection, and humiliation related to the trial and experience of divorce. The Blood of the Lamb covers divorce too!! I believe our predestined life (Romans 8:21-30, Romans 9:15-16) ordained by God, has purpose from beginning to end. My upbringing as a child in a Christian home with my mother and father helped to prepare me for my future trial as an adult.

While writing this section and allowing my daughter to read it she asked me, "What does all of this information have to do with helping women to become stronger while going through divorce?" I told her that my background needed to be understood so people could see the frame of reference that provided the foundation for my life and the way God used the foundation by His grace to strengthen me through the entire divorce trial..

Chapter I

My History

I never realized how my upbringing and childhood experiences would influence and even teach me how to manage my adult life. Most children never think about things like that because childhood is all about having fun. Growing up in Winnsboro, Louisiana in a small cotton and agricultural town in the northeastern part of the state where I and my Momma, Daddy, and my little brother lived, was a time when segregation was near its very end as law of the land. That little 'law' didn't seem to bother us because we always had fun riding to my maternal grandparent's home in Houston in our Model-T Ford with Momma and Daddy. My grandparents lived in an area of Houston called 5th Ward. That area and their former immaculate frame home has been replaced by the massive Houston interstate system. Grandma's home was filled with beautiful home-made lace curtains, original wood floors which were covered by woven floral wool rugs in the living and dinning rooms, one bath between the two bedrooms, a small kitchen, and front and back porches. Their lawn seemed to stay green and I can still smell the fragrance of deep pink crepe myrtles and dark plum/ magenta bachelor button flowers lining their front sidewalk. You might wonder what the point of these descriptions is. The point is that my upbringing had family order, wholeness, etc. and most people review the divorced coming from broken families, well I did not!

I lived with my grandparents for about a year and a half while Momma worked on her Masters in Music (piano and organ) and carried my soon to be little brother. My father worked daily to support us and eventually became the founding pastor Shiloh Baptist Church in Winnsboro. My Daddy named his church Shiloh because that was the name of his sweethearts' church (my Momma) in Houston.

My grandmother would take me with her to Shiloh Baptist Church (in Houston) choir practice each week and of course Sunday school and church services. Grandpa was a deacon at the same church. We would also have church trips to Galveston. I loved playing on the beach. Grandma was an excellent seamstress, cook, and could sew and design without a pattern. Grandma taught me how to use her treadle Singer sewing machine when I was about five years old and oh how we loved to shop for bargains at Foley's downtown. She was also a good singer and taught herself how to play piano. She also taught Momma and my mother's sister Aunt Bernice how to play piano with the small knowledge she had until she and Grandpa hired a professional to teach them advance piano.

Grandpa was independently employed as a truck driver and gas station owner. Grandpa loved to bring home snacks after work. Our favorite was Louisiana gumbo in a tall tin can filled with the aromas of gulf shrimp, vegetable seasonings (onion, garlic, and tomatoes), okra, and chicken. I also learned how to prepare Grandpa's favorite after work snack - pinto beans with raw onions on top. I moved back home with Momma and Daddy after Momma completed her Master's degree. I was about five years old at the time.

I became acquainted with death at age seven. I remember going to Grandma's house with all of my family. Momma, Daddy, my Aunt (Momma's sister) and her husband and Grandpa all gathered around Grandma who lay dying in her bed. She seemed so weak and frail but she was still very beautiful. I didn't understand why she seemed so weak. I would understand later that she was dying. I would later experience the same bedside family reunion around my Daddy's sickbed, then later at Grandpa's death. Grandpa (my mother's Dad) died in my family home in Winnsboro. He had come to live with us after he became ill in Houston.

Going to school riding in the car with my mother, who was a music teacher was exciting in those days. My Dad worked several jobs to provide for us along with my mothers' teaching salary. He was a school bus driver, laborer at the local cotton gin, and a Baptist pastor. I heard that Momma and Daddy had a cute romance history. The story goes that Momma and Daddy first met on her first teaching assignment at a Baptist seminary in Louisiana called Leland Seminary, where Daddy was enrolled. They married within the year. After their wedding in Mommy's home church, Shiloh Baptist in Houston's Fifth Ward, they returned to live in Winnsboro, LA and that's were Mommy raised us even after Daddy's death. Winnsboro was now Momma's home and she never returned to Texas except to visit relatives, taking us with her.

I was proud of my parents and enjoyed school. Even in our segregated community, most people knew my parents. You see we were not quite yet finished with the civil rights movement during this time. Daddy was known for his sense of humor, strong work ethic, and good character. Momma was known for the same but she was mostly known for her giftedness in music and her gentleness. During that time she was considered the most gifted piano and organ musician in our parish (*parish* for us is *county* in other states of the union). She played for most churches and had many private voice and piano students. We were a happy family with many paternal relatives in our small town. Momma and Daddy had help in rearing us. You see, in those days older people had some 'say so' in your upbringing. If you were caught doing something wrong they reported you immediately to your parents. I learned from my parents and the 'village' (all of those older folks helping to raise us) that hard work and using your gifts could supply extra income, and that a sense of responsibility would pay.

My brother and I were taught to drive at age 9 and 10. Daddy seemed to be driven to teach us many things at an early age. We were also in church "eight" days a week it seemed. Both my brother and I were in band (he played coronet and I the piano and saxophone), choir, 4-H, varsity basketball, FHA, and FFA. We weren't perfect children and Daddy disciplined us when necessary. He and Momma worked very hard to provide for us and we had good Christmases. Daddy purchased a good used sewing machine for me when I was about ten. I started making some of my clothes without a manufactured pattern and Daddy would give me money to buy fabric. We always enjoyed Christmas. Momma and Daddy always tried to get us at least one thing we hoped for.

Then during my early teens Daddy became ill. I remember long drives to the Veterans hospital in Alexandria, LA; it was about 110 miles away. Seeing Daddy lying in a hospital bed looking very weak and unable to recognize many people was frightening. Then on one occasion he looked in my direction, smiled, and said my name. I went over to him and held his hand and said, "Hi Daddy". That would be my last time to see my Daddy alive. It was a cold, gray, cloudy day in November when I was summoned at school to report for check out. I knew in my heart that it was about Daddy. For many years after that event, whenever it was cold, gray, and cloudy I would go into deep sadness and loneliness. I would try to hide this from Momma because I knew she now had the major responsibility of raising us by herself and I didn't want to add to her grief. She really missed Daddy but she kept us safe and stable in our little home in Winnsboro, LA.

My brother and I worked hard to make things run smoothly around the house in Daddy's absence. Brother (we were taught to call each other "Brother" and "Sister" and still do to this day) took care of the lawn, drove the car in for car maintenance and did other assigned chores. I cleaned the house and cooked the meals. We both shared the responsibility of taking out the garbage. This left time for Momma to teach private music lessons after school and practice the many church choirs she played for on varying Sunday's (churches in our community had designated services on 1st, 2nd, 3rd, and 4th Sunday's). I learned how to help Momma manage the household budget; I divided servings of food for the dinners that I prepared after school, and I cleaned the house. My brother and I were carrying some major adult responsibilities during our teenage years.

I graduated fifth in a class of seventy-seven students. My class would be next to the last segregated class to graduate in our parish. Our little town didn't suffer as much violence and cross burnings as other towns in the South. We basically had a smooth transition but many white private schools surfaced. Momma kept teaching in the public school system until she retired though she was reassigned to integrated schools. After graduation, I started my freshman year at Southern University and A. & M.

College, an 1890 college in Baton Rouge, designated for African Americans before integration.

I lived on campus and loved dormitory life for all four years of college. I went to school on state loans, Daddy's social security assistance and a small portion of VA funds. I carried the maximum class load each semester so I could finish as soon as possible and get a job. I worked two part-time jobs and went to Sunday school and church, football games and class. I would help Momma out with bills we had at home by sending some of my earnings from school. Holiday breaks were always exciting to me because I would go home to socialize and party with my hometown friends. I felt safe and secure when I returned home and at the time and I didn't have a steady boyfriend. While I was attending the university and living on campus, two students where shot and killed during a student protest standoff. I just felt safer going out at home than at school during those days.

One evening while working one of my part-time jobs as a dormitory resident assistant, I met my future husband. He was in uniform as a Marine reservist and was very handsome to me at the time. Our courtship would last for about two years. We married after I received which would be the first of three degrees that God would provide grace for me to earn. I took my first job in Shreveport, LA, a city about 250 miles from Baton Rouge my husband's hometown and returned one year later to Baton Rouge after accepting a job at the university as a Resident Counselor Director at my alma mater, Southern University. This job provided an apartment for us to live in while I worked, went to school at night to earn a Master's In Education. With my job, I also help put my husband through undergraduate school. Two years later I earned my Master's and my husband earned his Bachelor's; then I began to help my husband pursue his Master's. As a couple we seemed to be doing fine. I worked in several professional career positions during our marriage while my husband's employment included various blue-collar jobs and one white-collar position that didn't last long. After our first six years of marriage we had our first child, a little boy. Six years later we were blessed with a little girl. We were so proud and happy and both of us had earned master's degrees and were attending church together.

After eighteen years of marriage, homeownership, and strong church commitments my husband left for annual reserve summer camp as usual - but this time he never returned to our home. He then filed for legal separation, secured a divorce, and remarried with a church wedding within six months. This all happened while I was unsure of a job for the first time in my life, a job at my local church school ended. My husband knew about my job situation and left me with our children without any word or financial support. We'd never had a separation before in our marriage (although there were times I had valid suspicions). I thought how could this be? I helped put him through college. I worked while he went to college and now he was gone after eighteen years? I worked when he was let go from his job. Where was the support that I should receive from him as I'd given to him? I came to realize that I'd just experienced strikes one and two of the highest-ranking "severe human emotional stress" situations. No job and no husband. What is happening to my life? I would pray and cry out to God waiting for answers. What am I going to do to provide for my children?

The same type of fear and "gray cloud" loneliness crept in as when my Daddy died but I would pray and remember that if I worked hard just like Daddy taught me, train my children just as he and Momma did, and trust God, then I would get through this. Momma was still living at the time. She would come down to visit and bring such joy to my children and me. Momma, my aunt, my brother, and his wife, a best friend in California, and a few people from my church were my strongest support during this season of my life. God blessed me with a job within the public school system, which provided enough for me to maintain my mortgage and several other bills as well as pay the tithe each month according to the word of God.

I had to earn college credits to become certified in the area of special education. This process later led to my acceptance in the doctoral program and by God's grace and mercy earning a doctorate in Special Education. All of this studying kept my mind strong and focused. I received a pay increase after earning the doctorate. The increase in pay helped me to reduce and retire debt that I inherited from divorce during community property settlement. I conceded to this arrangement (debt inheritance from the marriage) in order to retain the domicile permanently in my name and the judge so ordered it. I prayed for wisdom and I believe that God impressed me to avoid as much strife as possible during the entire ordeal and this was a way to do it.

I felt that I needed to provide stability for my children in every area of our lives as much as possible. So, I remained in the same church, kept the same house, and created fun activities that didn't cost too much money. However, I could not afford to keep my children in private school any longer so I enrolled them in public schools. I secured a part-time job that allowed me to work from home. The extra income helped with debt reduction, childcare, and vacations. I kept a clean home, cooked the meals, helped with homework, purchased clothing on sale or used thrift- and garage- sale items to supply my growing children's needs. We were managing through the stress of divorce when, two years after that event, Momma became ill. She moved in with me and I cared for her on her last visit with us before she would go to heaven. This threw us into another void of loneliness, grief and depression. This was more of a struggle than the divorce for all three of us. I was now experiencing 'strike three', another severe human emotional stress event. It was just the grace of God that kept me with a sound mind and the strength to not give up. I would daily verbally confess I Tim. 1:7 (KJV): "For God hath not given us a spirit of fear; but of power, of love, and of a sound". I continued to keep our lives on schedule by maintaining stability in activities, nightly prayer and scripture in our home, and some recreation.

When it was time, I enrolled my children in driver's education because I didn't have time to personally teach them myself. I was able to give Momma's compact car to my son who was now age 15. I was blessed to have children who strived to do things right. Sometimes they were a little unruly but not too often. I think they didn't want to cause me grief. My son was heavily involved in our church youth ministry, played drums when he was very little, attained his first part-time job at age 16, graduated from high school and college, became a teacher and is serving God in his church. My daughter enjoyed high school. She served as president of her high school's Fellowship of Christian Students, sang in the choir, played piano and trumpet, taught children's church, graduated from college and now serves as a teacher and art photographer. The Lord blessed and provided resources for me to pay for my daughters' education free and clear. Then later on I was blessed to help retire my son's student loans. God was and still is faithful.

Looking back on the seasons of life that I have been allowed to experience I can say that God has truly blessed me to be able to live through all of the circumstances and severe human emotional stress issues that have come my way with some joy, peace, and success. All of the knowledge that I gained during my upbringing helped me to manage as a single mom. My advice to single mothers everywhere is to keep some form of stability in your children's lives and pray for them daily. Children can be just like baby birds: a warm familiar nest is better than a strange one if you can manage it. Also strive to be the best that you can. Improve your circumstances whenever you can. I haven't remarried. God has not sent the right person yet and the Lord keeps me content the way I am at the moment.

Now that you know my background, I want to share with you particular strategies and truths that God taught me that gave me victory and strength. It is my prayer that you will receive wisdom and strength for your journey and the trials of divorce and singleness. I'll start with overcoming fear and mind games and stress.

Points to Reflect on:

1. All of your earlier experiences in life can play a major role in your present life and future. Remember Romans 8: 28 And we know that all things work together for good to them that love God, to them who are the called according to his purpose.

2. Look for open doors of opportunity to increase and expand your professional life if possible. Let the Holy Spirit lead and guide you into new endeavors that can increase your resources. Remember Is. 54:2 Enlarge the place of thy tent, and let them stretch forth the curtains of thine habitations: spare not, lengthen thy cords, and strengthen thy stakes;

Chapter II

Becoming Strong in the Lord Facing Fear and Stress

2Timothy 1:5-7- When I call to remembrance the unfeigned faith that is in thee, which dwelt first in thy grandmother Lois, and thy mother Eunice; and I am persuaded that in thee also. 6Wherefore I put thee in remembrance that thou stir up the gift of God, which is in thee by the putting on of my hands. 7For God hath not given us the spirit of fear; but of power, and of love, and of a sound mind. (KJV)

I thank God for my godly mother and grandmother the late Mrs. Allie Payne Major and Mrs. Clara Labor Payne. As I mentioned earlier, both of these women provided a godly foundation in behavior and demeanor for my life. However, my trials differed from that of Momma's because my husband didn't die but deserted me which produced certain fears and stresses for the moments at hand. The timeline for my trials were as follows: July 1988, laid off from my teaching position, August 1988, desertion and abandonment, November 1988 served legal papers, May 1989 divorced, and July 1991 Momma went to be with the Lord. Events trials like these are bound to bring a certain amount of stress. Stress is defined in Webster's 1984 edition as: "force; pressure; strain; emphasis; weight or importance; accent; force producing change in shape or body". I want you to know and so does God that He will keep you and deliver you from stressful times that occur as a result of divorce.

Wouldn't you just know that stress could possibly force change in shape or body? All women should take note! Stress can come cause you to overeat as well as eat less than normal, thus causing the body to change shape and possibly healthy conditions. I learned to religiously take my daily dose of multiple vitamins and nutritional supplements. Not only can stress cause the body to change shape but the emotions, relationships with others, and ultimately the relationship with the Lord if prayer and fellowship with Him is not taken more seriously at this juncture in life.

God's grace allowed me to increase in my daily prayer time with an intensity to seek Him for every decision that I would make on a moment by moment basis, physical exercise, and academic study. That prayer time started every morning at 4am, a great while before my two children and the sun arose. I desperately needed the time alone with God to cry, mourn, seek His guidance for the day of work and rearing my children as a 'single mom'. I found myself quoting seemingly ritualistically "God has not given me a spirit of fear but of power and of love and of a sound mind" II Timothy 1:7. This one scripture was on autopilot for almost three years after I was deserted and abandoned. Why you may ask? Well, I've heard that too much stress and too many severe human emotional stress issues occurring simultaneously can cause a little 'craziness' on the brain (Ha, Ha)! But God did not allow that to happen to me!'. God knew, (but I didn't) that I needed more than ever soundness of mind due to the abnormal amounts of undiscovered stress, painful stigma attacks during sermons in church and among people who thought they just needed to pry and have something to say to me about my current life's situations. I was and still am kept daily by the power of the Lord Jesus' Holy Spirit and His word did not return void but it did accomplish that which He intended for it to do (So shall my word be that goeth forth out of my mouth: it shall not return unto me void, but it shall accomplish that which I please, and it shall prosper *in the thing* whereto I sent it. Isaiah 55:11 KJV), for me that was and still is to continue to have a sound mind. Soundness of my mind involved a structured, predictable, and ordered lifestyle.

Each night before bedtime I would lead my children in a Praise, Word, & Prayer time before sleep time. Each of us had to verbalize a blessing God provided from that day, then I would read scripture and discuss, next we would sing a song and pray. After that, we were all ready for bed. (Examples of child rearing were provided for me by my godly Mother as mentioned earlier. Daddy died when I was thirteen and I took on major responsibilities to help Momma out and so did my brother). This routine kept us with lifestyle expectations that evolved around the word of God, respect for Him on a daily basis, and a very strong work ethic. Our request in prayer would become our praise reports after the prayer was answered by the Lord. My children began to trust in the Lord more each day, and I became stronger each day by the power of the Holy Spirit.

In those days, I would prepare my two young children for school then prepare myself for work, see my eleven year old son off and drop my youngest (a little girl) off at daycare. The daycare center would take her to school and pick her up when school was out. This arrangement provided peace of mind and I did not worry about her safety while she was in first grade and while I was at work. My son was then in 7th grade and able to get on the bus and come home safely. The provisions God made for me to pay for child care was miraculous. My mother and brother helped out and God gave me wisdom in stretching my finances. Of course I continued to tithe on every increase God provided and He was always faithful. The spirit of joy increased while the spirit of heaviness decreased. This structured life continued all the way through my children's graduation from high school and college. I truly believe that God's provision and faithfulness to His word by giving me a sound mind and structured home environment provided the overcoming strength necessary in decreasing and eliminating accompanying stress.

Increasing my certifications in various areas of education required me to attend the university at night and I would bring my children with me. Tuition exemption was available for teachers certifying in critical shortage areas. God blessed me in that I did not have to pay for my education. All I had to do was study; keep my children with me, and work to provide for them while praying all the time. Learning to take advantage of open doors that increase stability and reduce fear became a priority in my life.

The other side of stress is fear. If allowed, divorce can paralyze with fear. In my case the fears were results of rejection, abandonment, slander, and a multitude of other acts of cruelty in and outside of the church. In the same manner, fear was defeated by speaking God's promises during my prayer and devotion times as well as choosing to abide and obey God's word to the best of my ability. Fear is not an easy thing to conquer. It's a moment by moment and second by second victory in the Lord. In every situation I learned to apply the courage God would give me for that particular moment or minute and move on in His will. Example, when I knew I had an assignment from God to do (such as sing, speak in public, or attend a gathering with believers who where married couples), my courage had to exponentially increase according to the event and situation. Why? Because unfortunately, some people do not accept you as they used to when you had a husband, so I learned to do what was right in Gods eyes, ignore the prejudice, mind my own business and do what was just and necessary for my family. The more I did what was necessary the less fear I had. God permitted me to become a lioness in the face of ridicule, snide looks, slander, and rejection. I no longer care what and who anyone thinks and why they think it. My concern is that I please God according to his word. I used to concern myself with other's perceptions of my life, but God continues to give me strength to cast down the imaginations in my mind about others perceptions of me. Learning and understanding who I am in Christ helped to eliminate that little problem. I am saved by God's grace; He loves me and let everyone work out their own salvation with fear and trembling. God did not give me or you a spirit of fear!

There were those who God sent my way who remembered to show concern and care for a woman like me. These were friends who stood by regardless of the situations I faced. They continued to invite me to some of their social functions and also included my children along with their children in their family events. I will never forget their compassion and help during those troubled times.

The timeline for blessings from God:

- August 1988 new job with a 200% pay increase; 1989,
- 4 additional certifications added to my teaching certificate;
- 1993, accepted to the Doctoral program;

- 1998 my son graduated from college; 2000 my daughter graduated from high school;
- I was re-baptized and made a stronger commitment to serve the Lord Jesus
- 2003 I graduated with my Doctorate and received another pay increase; 2005 my daughter graduated from college!!! God is faithful in making new and blessed timelines!!! Praise His Name!!!

Points to Reflect On:

1. Stay mindful of the types of food that you eat. Avoid stressful overeating and do look for healthy snacks. Apples, bananas, almonds, and walnuts are excellent crunchy foods to snack.
2. Increase and or focus your worship and prayer time with the Lord. His strength is made perfect in our weakness (II Corinthians 12:19).
3. Mutter scripture promises related to your situations daily, and especially when you are in a captive situation where words are being spoken that are opposed to the best God has for you and your children. The seed of the righteous is blessed, Ps. 112:2, the Lord is your husband and He will care for your (Is. 54)
4. Live an ordered and structured life. In other words be predictable as guided by the Holy Spirit for your journey. Let the Lord order your steps (Psalm 37:23) and allow Him to

order your steps in His word so you will not
sin against Him (Ps. 119:133).

5. Put your complete trust in God. Trust Him
with all of your heart (Proverbs 3:5-6).

Prayer and Confessions for Soundness of Mind

*Father, I praise you and thank you for your goodness
to my little ones and me. I come to you in the name of
Jesus. I thank you for all of the provisions you have
provided for my children and I today. I need your
strength and encouragement because I must have
your help to keep a sound mind. I remind you of your
word: "You have not given me a spirit of fear, but
of power and of love and of a sound mind". I thank
you for a sound mind and direction from your Holy
Spirit to make wise decisions today for my family.
You promised that you'd never leave me nor forsake
me, keep us safe and holy in Jesus name Amen.*

Chapter III

Becoming Strong in the Lord with Your Resources

Proverbs 23 *Be thou diligent to know the state of thy flocks, and look well to thy herds.*
24 *For riches are not for ever: and doth the crown endure to every generation?*
Proverbs 6: *[6]Go to the ant, thou sluggard; consider her ways, and be wise:[7]Which having no guide, overseer, or ruler,[8]Provideth her meat in the summer, and gathereth her food in the harvest.[9]How long wilt thou sleep, O sluggard? When wilt thou arise out of thy sleep?[10]Yet a little sleep, a little slumber, a little folding of the hands to sleep:[11]So shall thy poverty come as one that travelleth, and thy want as an armed man.*

Finances must be considered and managed with godly wisdom. I had to make necessary adjustments in spending patterns and if you are going through divorce or desertion you will too. Income from my former spouse was void and child support was nil during the initial stages of the desertion. Many times the answer to my children's request for material things was 'No'! They had to learn to adjust as well. My decisions for guiding my household became that of an 'authoritarian head of household Mom'! Responsibilities for our lives were left in my hands for some reason that God allowed and the decisions I made were final. Request that did not fit the budget were not honored but I would pray and ask God to meet our needs and desires.

As I prayed for wisdom in managing my finances, the Lord impressed me to list my utilities in my name and reduce expanded cable network programming to basic cable in order to fit my budget. My electricity would have been turned off by the company had I not followed the leading of the Lord by checking on my utilities and changing all other accounts to my name. I hadn't received current bills for a while and they would have become past due if I had not checked on them. One day while my little girl was watching Sesame Street, the screen went dark. She began to cry so I called the cable company and explained my current domestic situation, made a request that they change the account to my name and that I would be responsible for the bills. The company representative was very cooperative and did what I asked. I believe that was the favor of God and my little girl would continue to see Sesame Street. To see the smile on her little face meant so much to me. I truly believe my heavenly Father was just as pleased.

As I continued daily to request strength, wisdom, and finances from the Lord, extra help would come from my brother and his wife and my mother. The scripture that God spoke to me concerning managing my finances was and still is Proverbs 27:23- "Be thou diligent to know the state of thy flocks, and look well to thy herds" (KJV). In those days I knew the exact amount in my checking account, which checks had not cleared yet, and continuously scribbled my budget and expenditures on scratch sheets of paper (scribbling my budget became a method of relieving boredom during some professional meetings, and through sermons that lacked the anointing). God blessed me with a new job that nearly tripled my take home pay and I was able to tithe, pay my mortgage, utilities and monthly payments on the bills left over from the marriage. I inherited all of the bills from the marriage in exchange for the marital domicile and mortgage being placed legally and completely in my name and ownership. This was yet another way God allowed me to keep my children in a safe and structured environment. The new job replaced the former Christian private school teaching job. With the new job and increased pay God enabled me to live in the home my children knew as their family home.

The gift of managing finances was prevalent throughout my life and God continued to increase my abilities. It is important to 'know the state of your flocks'. This scripture from Proverbs related to my financial accounts (checking, savings, investments, etc.). Creative ways for extending a dollar was ever present on my mind and the Holy Spirit opened the doors for such creativity.

I have lots of advice to give towards extending the dollar and maintaining a budget while living within your means but my advice is only good when it's founded on God's word. Hebrews 13:5 says: "⁵Let your conversation be without covetousness; and be content with such things as ye have: for he hath said, I will never leave thee, nor forsake thee. Contentment is one of the main ingredients in managing your resources. Look at your expenses and identify what you can live without! Sometimes there are unnecessary luxuries such as: gym memberships, full program cable television service, membership dues for large box stores, credit cards with annual fees (get rid of them as soon as possible), etc. Utilize the public library as free entertainment and eliminate monthly subscriptions. You can even read the local newspaper for free in the library and use free internet services wherever you can. Create your own health fitness program at home or use free local walking and running tracks and parks. Free programs like these can be found in some local churches, schools, and parish/county recreation centers. Don't forget to use vintage stores for classic clothes at bargain prices if you need additional clothes. Now, become content with what God has allowed you to have for now.

Different people have varying ways of handling their money, but I believe if I pay a certain portion of my money (the tithe) to God first as stated Old Testament book of Malachi 3:10 and additional offerings as you are able, God will then bless your finances.

He truly blessed mine. Over the many years since the desertion and divorce, God has increased my personal finances and I do give Him all of the praise, honor, and glory! However, only God can provide good doctors reports and health, a sound mind, and favor with others. These are blessing and resources that cannot be purchased but can be prayed for and expressed through our confessions of Gods promises. A physician can provide diagnosis, prescriptions, etc. but only God can provide and extend life to your body.

Points to Reflect on:

1. Put God first in your finances. Strengthen your obedience in this area. Do your very best to tithe according to Malachi 3:10. This means 10% of your earnings before taxes. If not possible at the moment, start where you can and make an arrangement with God to increase as He increases your finances.
2. Serve God with your time and talents. Place Him first in all things.
3. Learn to be content with such things that you have (Heb. 13: 5-6) and avoid being consumed by the love of money.
4. Have a budget, a planned way of spending and saving. Even ants know how to work and save (Pro. 6:6-11).
5. Prioritize your needs and desires. Be careful how you live. Make the most of every oppor-

tunity (Ephesians. 5:15-16). Seek God's kingdom first (Matthew 6:33).

6. Believe the promises and stand and believe them each and every day of your life and become STRONG in your faith!!!

Prayer for becoming a strong manager of your resources:

Lord, you are the only one who really knows all about my resources and my material, physical, and spiritual needs. You are aware of everything regarding my children's needs and all of my concerns. I believe your word and stand on your promises in Isaiah 53:5 "But he was wounded for our transgressions, he was bruised for our iniquities: the chastisement of our peace was upon him; and with his stripes we are healed" and in Luke 6:38" Give, and it shall be given unto you; good measure, pressed down, and shaken together, and running over, shall men give into your bosom. For with the same measure that ye mete withal it shall be measured to you again". So Lord, I give to others and expect you to bless me as you said, I believe you for divine health and peace of mind. Give me wisdom, strength, and the necessary tools to become a strong manager of all of my resources. Let all of the talents and gifts you created in me be used glorify you and you alone. Help me to always remember and give to the poor and needy, and let me always put you first in my giving. Increase the joy I have in giving, in Jesus name amen.

Chapter IV

Becoming Strong in the Lord in the Face of Slander

Psalm 41:5 *Mine enemies speak evil of me, when shall he die, and his name perish?*

What is slander? My definition of slander is a lie that is spoken which is generally demeaning against someone's character or reputation. Slander can be very ugly and demeaning, especially when it comes from your 'Sisters and Brothers' in Christ. This type of trial made me think of praying some of David's prayers for his enemies. Thinking about the reward for unrepentant slandering might just bring you some satisfaction. After all, all liars will have their place in the lake of fire! But hey, you really wouldn't want that to happen to anyone, so repent if you're thinking about that, I did! Divorce, especially if you are a Christian when it happens to you affords opportunities for some folks to 'give up' a little slander on your name. That happened to me on several occasions. Reflecting on some of the slander and gossip spoken against me (and of course people make sure you hear about it, even in the church) brings back memories of anger, disgust, and near hatred, but today that's a different story. You see, God has healed my heart and delivered me from that which is past and I have forgiven those people. The anguish is gone! Forgiveness came immediately in the throne room of God but forgetting and learning to laugh about it took some time, yes lots of time.

The enemy of our soul and spirit uses any tactic he can to discourage our walk of faith in the Lord Jesus and his keeping power through promises in his word. People are used by Satan to spread lies and help his cause to distract a wounded sheep and destroy if possible. There were many times I wanted to pray particular people away and hoped they'd hurry and drop off into the lake of fire where all liars will go one day. But, I could not do that because the word of God declares that I must forgive in order to be forgiven. Accusations against my character are what I hated most. Why? Because goals set for my life did not agree at all with the accusers lies. My face then became set like a flint to live above those particular lies!! Examples of various types of slander/lies that I endured include but were not limited to were arrogance, bankruptcy after the divorce, remarriage twice after the divorce, leaving the church where I served for many years, the list could go on and on but that's enough for any reader to view. I have peace now because I know that God is always in control and just maybe the circumstances increased my strength in God's power and faithfulness. Divorce does not surprise God even when it happens to one of his own. It amazes me that scripture references of divorce were spoken to the religious sect, and new believers in the New Testament, not unsaved people! Many that come to mind are: Matthew 5:31 and 19:7, Mark 10:9, I Corinthians 7:10-11 and I Corinthians 12 – 24. I'll not do a sermon on the reasons for divorce because you can read for yourself. However, the Bible clearly states that unfaithfulness is grounds for divorce and if the unbeliever chooses to leave then the remaining spouse if free to remarry only in the Lord! Who will determine if a person is truly a believer? Only God knows what's in each individual's heart. A day of reckoning will come for everyone one day!

Many of today's sermons rivet cruelty to those who have experienced divorce... Some media/television sermons admonishing wives to just not sleep with (have physical intimacy) their husbands when the husband has been unfaithful!! Really, everybody needs a break on that line! Let's see, in a society where killer STD's are running rampant the preacher wants the women of his church to just lay there with the adulterer? I believe that's why the Lord and Paul gave the reasons for divorce. They knew thousands of years ago that HIV and AIDS and all of the other known STD's could cause death. The causes of divorce between each couple will be weighed out in eternity on God's scales of justice, redemption, mercy, and grace, not the words of slanders, gossips, and the ill informed. God taught me how to be at peace and grow strong in face of the slanderers, gossips, and ill informed.

The scripture tells us that God knows the deepest longings of our heart; He knows how we feel when we are lied on. He was lied on himself but forgave. We must forgive in order to become stronger in the Lord and to move on in Christ

Points to Reflect on:

1. God is your judge. You will stand before Him and give an account for the deeds done in this body while you are on planet earth. Your sins have been washed away by the blood of Jesus Christ (I John 1:7)
2. No one has the right to slander you but you must forgive and move on to become STRONG! Who can charge you with anything (Romans 8:33)? God is your judge.
3. Pray that slanderers will not to be established in the land (Ps. 140:11). Walk with your head held high in the power and STRENGTH of the Holy Spirit (Ps. 119:80).

Prayer for mercy on those who spitefully slander and demean us:

Lord Jesus, you have seen how I have been lied on and it hurts. You said that I could ask the Father anything in your name and He would do it according to your word (And this is the confidence that we have in him that, if we ask any thing according to his will, he heareth us: I John 5:14). It is your will that I have joy, peace, a clean heart, and love for others. Cleanse my heart from anguish and bitterness related to slander against me. I forgive those who have slandered me and I confess your word over my life that "No weapon that is formed against thee shall prosper; and every tongue that shall rise against thee in judgment thou shalt condemn. This is the heritage of the servants of the LORD, and their righteousness is of me, saith the LORD. Isaiah 54:17). Protect and keep me holy by the power of your word and the Holy Spirit, in Jesus name I pray, Amen.

Chapter V

Becoming Stronger and Wiser in Relationships

Proverbs 18: 24-A man/woman that hath friends must shew himself friendly: and there is a friend that sticketh closer than a brother. I **Corinthians 15: 33** Be not deceived: evil communications corrupt good manners. **Proverbs 27:6** Faithful are the wounds of a friend; but the kisses of an enemy are deceitful. 7 The full soul loatheth an honeycomb; but to the hungry soul every bitter thing is sweet. *I Corinthians 15:11 But now I have written unto you not to keep company, if any man that is called a brother be a fornicator, or covetous, or an idolater, or a railer, or a drunkard, or an extortioner; with such an one no not to eat.*

Our Christian faith is built on the relationship we have with Christ Jesus as Lord and savior. Every Christian (in my opinion) is still growing daily in God's wisdom in areas of spiritual and natural relationships. Godly relationships must be built on the foundation of God's word. As a Christian we are in the world (just passing though) but not of the world. Romans 12:2 -And be not conformed to this world: but be ye transformed by the renewing of your mind, that ye may prove what is that good, and acceptable, and perfect, will of God. Maintaining godly friendships during the trials of divorce affords the opportunity to see who your real friends are and evaluate why you choose certain people as friends. Life is too short to be concerned and offended when some people don't treat you as friendly as they did while you were married. God has good plans for our lives, even though the trials maybe hellish! Godly friendships are a blessing from God and I was and still am blessed with many godly friends. The enemy of our souls will try to send counterfeit friends in our way. Sometimes friendships seem to be seasonal and each phase of my life had a different set of friends. Not that they were not friendly all of the time but their assignment in my life had seasons. I believe that friendships have designated seasons of closeness and usefulness from God in our lives. When the season is over one must be careful not to feel rejected by their friend(s). The Lord taught me this through prayer and personal examination that He allows particular people in our lives for a season.

Visiting an older mentor who I admired as a child and who encouraged me in my professional aspirations all through college and young adulthood often provided sound advice. When the trial of desertion, abandonment, and divorce came my way and I shared my heart with her about how I prayed to remain faithful to the Lord and to stay physically holy and pure she responded, "I hope you fall". I was deeply hurt and devastated and that was the last time I visited her for any length of time. Her season of encouragement ended with the ungodly admonition. Having the strength from God is necessary in our lives when we must separate from anyone who desires our demise spiritually, physically, or emotionally. Reduce phone calls, visits, and any form of contact to null and void. Pleasantries can be exchanged when unavoidable. I forgave her and wondered with a hurting heart why she would say something like that. Moving on in life takes strength from God which he provided for me. Just as this woman wanted to provide corrupt communications there were many other friends who encouraged me to press onward in the Lord even (Ephesians 5:11 And have no fellowship with the unfruitful works of darkness, but rather reprove *them*.) though my trials were fierce at the time.

I became very guarded around the opposite sex. It appeared to me that some men felt that divorced women were on the 'hunt' so I stopped initiating any conversations with men. I sincerely was not interested (even though it appeared to me that some think too highly of themselves when they imagine someone would even be interested). I didn't and don't think too highly of myself in that area and continue to walk with God cautiously in this area of my life.

After six years of legal singleness I developed a long distance relationship with a gentleman from another state. Having someone send me flowers, cards and gifts made me feel like a teenager all over again. The only problem was, was that I did not consult the Lord about the matter. After many months of long distance courtship and dating (when possible) the relationship seemingly took a serious turn into marriage possibilities. Having served in the same church for many years I confided in my pastor. I was stunned when the pastor began to pray for God's keeping power for me and bind the devil off of my life! The immediate emotion was disappointment and sadness. My pastor sent inquires to the church where this man fellowshipped and the reports were not too favorable. Thank God for a concerned pastor. My relationship eventually ended with this man and I continued to pursue my studies towards the Doctorate in Special Education. Why did this happen to me?

The full soul loatheth an honeycomb; but to the hungry soul every bitter thing is sweet Proverbs, 27:7. This scripture (to me) can represent the eagerness for companionship without being fully satisfied in the joy of the Lord. Caution and prayer must be exercised before attempting to enter the dating and courtship arena. Things have changed in that arena over the years and I was married for 18 years then single again. Most probably I could have been classified as a neophyte in the dating scene, after all the dating experience for me had not occurred for 24 years. Contentment with the state that I find myself in (a single, god fearing, blood washed walking in holiness Christian female) has arrived and I have never remarried. That's not to say that others who have experienced life as I have will have the same philosophy, but I am satisfied. Bottom line is: pray diligently before making any attempt to involve yourself again. You could be leaping from the frying pan into a much hotter skillet! There are many scriptures to advise anyone on marriage.

I Corinthians 7:39 The wife is bound by the law as long as her husband liveth; but if her husband be dead, she is at liberty to be married to whom she will; only in the Lord. I Corinthians 7:15 But if the unbelieving depart, let him depart. A brother or a sister is not under bondage in such cases: but God hath called us to peace. Or course the Lord Jesus said in Matthew 19:9 And I say unto you, whosoever shall put away his wife, except *it be* for fornication, and shall marry another, committeth adultery: and whoso marrieth her which is put away doth commit adultery. Wisdom and guidance through prayer must be made to see if a person qualifies to remarry according to the scriptures mentioned previously. Determining your qualifications should be confirmed by the Holy Spirit, your pastor or some other godly person that you allow yourself to be accountable to. Each of us will have to give an account to God for the deeds done in this body and remember, Romans 8:28 and we know that all things work together for good to them that love God, to them who are the called according to his purpose. There is therefore now no condemnation to them which are in Christ Jesus, who walk not after the flesh, but after the Spirit (Romans 8:1). The key is to continue to walk in the Spirit of

God while making no provisions for the flesh to sin, continuous prayer for strength in God and direction in godly relationships.

Another good passage that can help visualize the seriousness of relationships and deceptions can be taken from Proverbs 7. I know many might think Proverbs 7 is all about a man avoiding a promiscuous woman. The New Testament provides insight as to how God looks at all of us. Galatians 3:28 says: "There is neither Jew nor Greek, there is neither bond nor free, there is neither male nor female: for ye are all one in Christ Jesus. Let's adapt Proverbs 7 to advice to a daughter instead of a son. It would probably read like this:

Points to Reflect on:

1. Let the Lord heal you from the trial and wounds of divorce before you even consider becoming involved in a dating or courtship relationship. God will hear and comfort you if you cry out to him (Ps. 37:17-20). John 14:27 declares that Jesus leaves you peace. He will provide you with the calmness you need to become STRONG IN HIM!
2. Ask God for wisdom in choosing friends. Your close circle of friends should be prayerfully considered. Ask God for his wisdom (James 1:5).
3. Read Proverbs 7 as if it was written to the kings' daughter.

Proverbs 7 (Written to a young woman)

My daughter keep my words, and lay up my commandments with thee.

²Keep my commandments, and live; and my law as the apple of thine eye.

³Bind them upon thy fingers, write them upon the table of thine heart.

⁴Say unto wisdom, Thou art my sister; and call understanding thy kinswoman:

⁵That they may keep thee from the strange man, from the stranger which flattereth with his words.

⁶For at the window of my house I looked through my casement,

⁷And beheld among the simple ones, I discerned among the youths, a young woman void of understanding,

⁸Passing through the street near his corner; and she went the way to his house,

⁹In the twilight, in the evening, in the black and dark night:

¹⁰And, behold, there met her a man with the attire of an whoremonger/adulterer, and cunning of heart.

¹¹(He is loud and stubborn; his feet abide not in his house:

¹²Now is he without, now in the streets, and lieth in wait at every corner.)

¹³So he caught her, and kissed her, and with an impudent face said unto her,

¹⁴I have money with me; this day have I paid my tithes and offerings.

[15]Therefore came I forth to meet you, diligently to seek thy face, and I have found thee.

[16]I have prepared my home and decorated it with the finest of furnishings from the best stores in town.

[17]I have perfumed my bed with myrrh, aloes, and cinnamon.

[18]Come, let us take our fill of love until the morning: let us solace ourselves with loves.

[19]For you don't know that I'm married and my wife is not at home, she is gone a long journey:

[20]She hath taken a bag of money with her, and will come home at the day appointed.

[21]With his much manly speech he caused her to yield, with the flattering of his mouth he forced her.

[22]She goeth after him straightway, as an ox goeth to the slaughter, or as a fool to the correction of the stocks;

[23]Till a dart strike through her liver; as a bird hasteth to the snare, and knoweth not that it is for her life.

[24]Hearken unto me now therefore, O ye children, and attend to the words of my mouth.

[25]Let not thine heart decline to his ways, go not astray in his paths.

[26]For he hath cast down many wounded: yea, many strong women have been slain by him.

[27]His house is the way to hell, going down to the chambers of death.

Prater for God strength and wisdom in relationships:

Father, I again approach your throne with thanksgiving and a need. Thank you for my salvation and infilling of your Holy Spirit. Your word declares that I am kept by the power of the Holy Spirit and without holiness no one will see God. Continuously strengthen me to abide in your power and presence, give me wisdom in all relationships on this planet, and let me live my life according to your word, in Jesus name amen.

Final Prayer: Salvation

God in heaven, I believe that Jesus Christ is your son and you sent him to earth to die for my sins. He was born of virgin birth and was not conceived by natural causes. He lived a sinless life, was crucified on a cross, bled and died, was buried, and arose from the grave just for me. He is alive in heaven with you seated at your right hand praying just for me right now. Lord Jesus, forgive me of all my sins and come into my heart. Be my Lord and savior all of my days and help me to serve you all of my life by the power of your Holy Spirit. Amen.

Now you must begin to read your Bible daily and have discussions with God. These discussions are called prayer. Before you begin to read, ask God to help you understand what you are reading and speak to your personally through His word in Jesus name.

Seek God's direction in locating a Bible teaching church that will build your faith and strengthen your walk with God.

Dedications

Now it's time for me to give honor to which honor is due, those who helped me along the way of my journey. Those who never failed to help when it was their season to help. May God remember them and show mercy on them in His kingdom to come.

1. Tipp M. & Helen Major – my brother and his wife for all of the love, care, provisions and compassion they could possibly give. For the many summer vacations they gave my children and for the sister –in-law who is like the sister I never had.
2. Mrs. Allie Payne Major (Hagan) – my late mother who gave her all for me and God blessed me to care for during her home going illness.
3. Mr. William & Mrs. Elsie Major – my late aunt and uncle from my small rural home-

town. The door and pots were always open with lots of love and laughter.

4. Mrs. Bernice Boney – my late aunt who encouraged me diligently to pursue the terminal degree and always had a godly word to say.

5. Mrs. Gladys Moore – a kind hearted saint who never demeans but always has a gentle word of care and concern. She also helped with my little girl when I needed someone to watch for a few moments.

6. Mrs. Sharon Brown – a friend who provided safe care for my daughter by allowing her housekeeper to watch my child along with hers in her home during the most vulnerable years of a little girl's life.

7. Mrs. Ruth Stockstill- The late wife of the founding pastor of my church. I could share my heart with her. She was filled with godly wisdom and compassion, Sister Ruth gave me encouraging words and grocery gift cards during the holidays. Those gift cards continued then stopped when God increased my financial resources.

8. Mrs. Agnes Major Hicks – my late aunt who gave insight and encouragement doing the hard times. She was a magnificent self-taught artist.

9. State Senator Sharon W. Broome - a friend for 30+ years, who remembered to include me many events and never made me feel like an outsider.

10. Nancy Sue Gregorie, Attorney – a dedicated person who stuck with me for 9 years in court proceedings.
11. Mrs. Gwen Bruton – my immediate supervisor at a small school. She was blunt, funny, and red headed but could make you laugh by speaking ordinarily. She served as a comfort when I was served divorce papers on my job.
12. Mrs. Jackie LaCour – and her husband would include my little girl on trips with their daughter. She also threw a great graduation party for me when I received the Doctorate.
13. Mrs. Barbara Thomas – and her husband (both are now pastors) provided many activities for my children and I during those trying days of my mothers' illness and home-going. Barbara also helped to care for my Mom doing her home-going illness.
14. Mrs. Ethel Veal – her husband (both are now pastors) came to my home in the early days of the desertion and watched for my children to get off of the bus and let them in the house until I could arrive from work. May God always give you favor.
15. Dr. Carol Deaton, Dr. Carol Pearson, and the late Mrs. Beulah Clark – professors who helped me through the Doctoral program process
16. Andy and Dorcas (my children) – Hanging in there while 'Mommy" did the best she could to provide by God's grace/

References

1. Allee, J. G., PhD. (1984). *Webster's dictionary.* Chicago. Wilcon & Follett Book Company.
2. Scripture quotations in this publication are from the King James Version of the Bible.

CPSIA information can be obtained
at www.ICGtesting.com
Printed in the USA
LVHW091511051021
699577LV00006B/241

9 781622 301751